THE OFFICIAL

BOB'S BURGERS™

GUIDED
JOURNAL

First published in the United States of America in 2018
by UNIVERSE PUBLISHING, a division of
Rizzoli International Publications, Inc.
300 Park Avenue South
New York, NY 10010
www.rizzoliusa.com

Design by Celina Carvalho
Printed in Hong Kong, PRC

2018 2019 2020 2021 2022 / 10 9 8 7 6 5 4 3 2 1

ISBN-13: 978-0-7893-3449-7
Library of Congress Control Number: 2018904125

THE OFFICIAL
BOB'S BURGERS ™

GUIDED
JOURNAL

FROM THE CREATORS OF *BOB'S BURGERS*

UNIVERSE

I AM A SMART, STRONG, SENSUAL

YOUR NAME HERE

IF I WERE IN A RAP BATTLE WITH MY SO-CALLED "IMAGINARY" FRIEND KEN, THESE ARE THE LYRICS I WOULD IMPROVISE . . .

_____

_____

_____

_____

_____

_____

_____

_____

_____

_____

_____

_____

_____

_____

_____

_____

_____

_____

THE STORE I WOULD OPEN NEXT TO BOB'S BURGERS THAT WOULD ALMOST IMMEDIATELY GO OUT OF BUSINESS IS . . .

_____

_____

_____

_____

_____

_____

_____

_____

_____

_____

_____

_____

_____

_____

_____

_____

_____

_____

_____

THE LAST CRAP ATTACK I HAD WAS . . .

_____

_____

_____

_____

_____

_____

_____

_____

_____

_____

_____

_____

_____

_____

_____

_____

_____

_____

_____

_____

_____

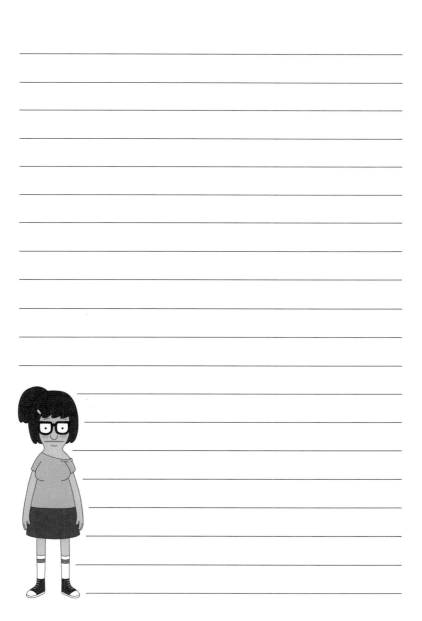

IF I HAD A GANG OF CATS TRAINED TO DO MY BIDDING, THEY WOULD BE NAMED . . .

MY ONE THOUSAND, THREE HUNDRED AND FIFTY-FOUR BURGER OF THE DAY IDEAS ARE . . .

_____

_____

_____

_____

_____

_____

_____

_____

_____

_____

_____

_____

_____

_____

_____

_____

_____

_____

_____

_____

THIS IS AN ACCURATE ACCOUNT OF HOW I MET
MY IMAGINARY HORSE . . .

_____

_____

_____

_____

_____

_____

_____

_____

_____

_____

_____

_____

_____

_____

_____

_____

_____

_____

IF I WERE TO WRITE A MUSICAL
TO BE PERFORMED IN A SCHOOL'S BOILER ROOM,
IT WOULD BE ABOUT . . .

_____

_____

_____

_____

_____

_____

_____

_____

_____

_____

_____

_____

_____

_____

_____

_____

_____

_____

_____

_____

_____

_____

I BELIEVE A SNAKE'S LACK OF ARMS AND LEGS IS
(A) OKAY
(B) NOT OKAY, AND HERE'S WHY . . .

_____

_____

_____

_____

_____

_____

_____

_____

_____

_____

_____

_____

_____

_____

IF I COULD FLUSH ANYTHING DOWN MY OUTSIDE TOILET, IT WOULD BE . . .

_____

_____

_____

_____

_____

_____

_____

_____

_____

_____

_____

_____

_____

_____

_____

_____

_____

_____

_____

_____

I THINK THE IDEAL PLACE TO KEEP A GHOST IS . . .

_____

_____

_____

_____

_____

_____

_____

_____

_____

_____

_____

_____

_____

_____

_____

_____

_____

_____

_____

IF I WERE LUCKY ENOUGH TO BE ASKED OUT BY A ZOMBIE, OUR DREAM DATE WOULD BE . . .

_____

_____

_____

_____

_____

_____

_____

_____

_____

_____

_____

_____

_____

_____

_____

_____

_____

_____

LOBSTERS ARE GROSS. IF I COULD GIVE A LOBSTER A PIECE OF MY MIND, I WOULD SAY . . .

I WOULD FILL OUT THE ONLINE DATING PROFILE OF MY FAVORITE MORTICIAN LIKE THIS . . .

_____

_____

_____

_____

_____

_____

_____

_____

_____

_____

_____

_____

_____

_____

_____

_____

_____

_____

_____

_____

I WOULD WIN ANY COSTUME CONTEST
IF I DRESSED AS A . . .

_____

_____

_____

_____

_____

_____

_____

_____

_____

_____

_____

_____

_____

_____

_____

_____

_____

_____

_____

HERE ARE THE LENGTHS MY FAMILY AND I WOULD GO TO IN ORDER TO WIN A SUPERCOOL MINIVAN . . .

_____

_____

_____

_____

_____

_____

_____

_____

_____

_____

_____

_____

_____

_____

_____

_____

_____

_____

_____

_____

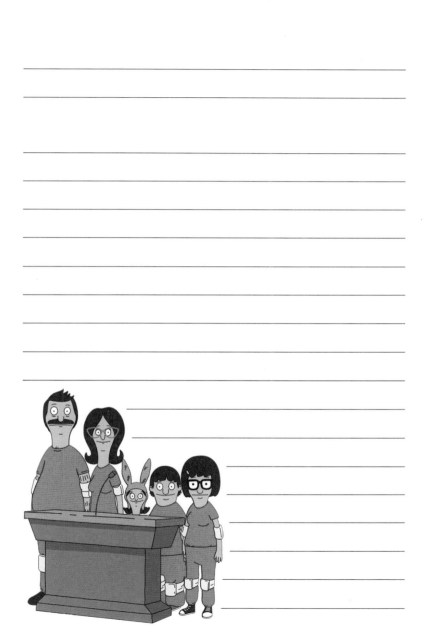

I WOULD LET MY PARENT TEACH ME THIS IN ORDER TO GET OUT OF GOING TO GYM . . .

_____

_____

_____

_____

_____

_____

_____

_____

_____

_____

_____

_____

_____

_____

_____

_____

_____

_____

THE BAND MEMBER THAT I WOULD MOST LIKE TO SLAP AND WHY (AS IF IT WEREN'T OBVIOUS) IS . . .

_____

_____

_____

_____

_____

_____

_____

_____

_____

THE GAME THAT I WOULD MOST LIKE TO PLAY UNTIL I GO INSANE AND THINK I AM LITERALLY IN THAT GAME IS . . .

_____

_____

_____

_____

_____

_____

_____

_____

_____

_____

_____

_____

_____

_____

_____

_____

_____

_____

MY FORT WOULD HAVE THE FOLLOWING ROOMS, IN ADDITION TO A FARTING ROOM . . .

_____

_____

_____

_____

_____

_____

_____

_____

_____

_____

_____

_____

_____

_____

_____

_____

_____

_____

_____

IF I WERE A TERRIBLE SCHOOL GUIDANCE COUNSELOR, MY THERAPY DOLLS WOULD BE NAMED . . .

_____

_____

_____

_____

_____

_____

_____

_____

_____

_____

_____

_____

_____

_____

_____

_____

_____

_____

DOODLE WALL OF NO JUDGMENT

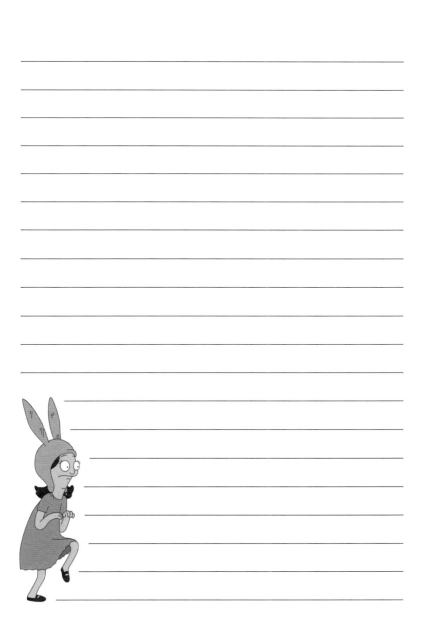

THE HAUNTED HOUSE I WOULD DESIGN
TO TERRIFY MY CHILDREN WOULD INCLUDE . . .

_____

_____

_____

_____

_____

_____

_____

_____

_____

_____

_____

_____

_____

_____

_____

_____

_____

_____

_____

_____

_____

THIS HOLIDAY HAS BEEN GROSSLY OVERLOOKED
FOR ITS MUSICAL POTENTIAL, SO I WROTE A
SONG ABOUT IT . . .

_____

_____

_____

_____

_____

_____

_____

_____

_____

_____

THE ONLY WAY I COULD TOP A THREE BEAN SALAD PARTY WOULD BE WITH THIS KIND OF PARTY . . .

_____

_____

_____

_____

_____

_____

_____

_____

_____

_____

_____

_____

_____

_____

_____

_____

_____

_____

_____

IF I WERE TO WEAR A MASK TO TERRORIZE A MORNING TALK SHOW, MY ALTER EGO IN THAT SCENARIO WOULD BE . . .

_____

_____

_____

_____

_____

_____

_____

_____

_____

_____

_____

_____

_____

_____

THE THREE OTHER MEMBERS OF MY BAND, GIRLZ 4 NOW, ARE AS FOLLOWS, ALONG WITH OUR FIRST THREE HIT SONGS . . .

_____

_____

_____

_____

_____

_____

_____

_____

_____

_____

_____

_____

_____

_____

_____

_____

HERE'S WHAT I WOULD NAME THE RACCOONS IN MY ALLEY IF THEY APPROACHED ME AND ASKED FOR MY HELP . . .

IF I CAME ACROSS SOME WHALE POOP AND/OR VOMIT, HERE'S WHAT I'D DO WITH IT, AFTER SNEAKING A QUICK TASTE . . .

_____

_____

_____

_____

_____

_____

_____

_____

_____

_____

_____

_____

_____

_____

_____

_____

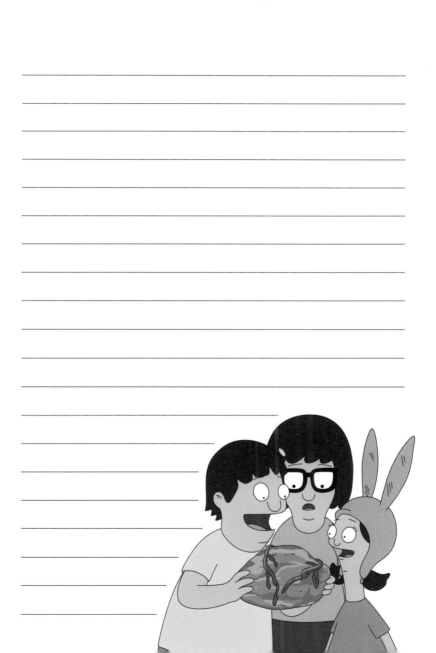

IF I HAD A CRAZY FEVER DREAM, THESE ARE THE TOYS I'D WANT TO SHOW UP TO FIGHT AND/OR GO ON AN ADVENTURE WITH . . .

_____

_____

_____

_____

_____

_____

_____

_____

_____

_____

_____

_____

_____

_____

_____

_____

BELOW I HAVE DRAWN VARIOUS FOOD ITEMS WITH ANGRY FACES

IF I STOLE MR. AMBROSE'S YOGURT, HERE'S HOW I'D GET AWAY WITH IT . . .

_____

_____

_____

_____

_____

_____

_____

_____

_____

_____

_____

_____

_____

_____

_____

_____

_____

THE TYPE OF CANDY THAT I WOULD YELL AT THE CANDY COMPANY BOARD MEMBERS NEVER TO CHANGE IS . . .

_____

_____

_____

_____

_____

_____

_____

_____

_____

_____

_____

_____

_____

_____

_____

_____

_____

IF I COULD WEAR A HAT EVERY DAY AND NEVER TAKE IT OFF, EVEN AT THE POOL, IT WOULD LOOK LIKE . . .

_____

_____

_____

_____

_____

_____

_____

_____

_____

_____

_____

_____

_____

_____

_____

_____

_____

_____

MY THREE NEW EQUESTRANAUT CHARACTERS THAT EVERYONE AT NEXT YEAR'S EQUESTRA-CON WILL BE IN COSTUME AS ARE . . .

_____

_____

_____

_____

_____

_____

_____

_____

THE ONE THING I WOULD CHAIN MYSELF TO, SWALLOW THE KEY, AND NOT POOP IT OUT FOR IS . . .

_____

_____

_____

_____

_____

_____

_____

_____

_____

_____

_____

_____

_____

_____

_____

_____

_____

_____

IF I HAD TO WRITE A STORY ABOUT AUNT GAYLE IN ORDER TO GET TO GO TO YARNIVAL WITH HER, IT WOULD BE . . .

_____

_____

_____

_____

_____

_____

_____

                           _____

                           _____

                           _____

                           _____

                           _____

                           _____

                           _____

IF I WERE TRYING OUT FOR THE WAGSTAFF WHALERS CHEERLEADING SQUAD, THIS IS THE GROUNDBREAKING CHEER I'D WOW EVERYONE WITH . . .

_____

_____

_____

_____

_____

_____

_____

_____

_____

_____

_____

_____

_____

_____

_____

_____

_____

_____

_____

TRUST ME, THE BEST PLACE TO HIDE A ROTTEN EASTER EGG IN MY HOUSE IS . . .

I'VE DONE SO MANY NICE THINGS THIS YEAR,
SANTA. HERE THEY ARE IN HELPFUL
SONG FORM . . .

_____

_____

_____

_____

_____

_____

_____

_____

_____

_____   _____   _____

_____

_____

IF I WERE RUNNING FOR CLASS PRESIDENT JUST SO MY NEMESIS DOESN'T WIN, SOME OF MY SLOGANS WOULD BE . . .

_____

_____

_____

_____

_____

_____

_____

_____

_____

_____

_____

_____

_____

_____

_____

_____

_____

WHEN BABYSITTING A POSSESSED, CROTCH-KICKING CHILD, ONE MUST . . .

_____

_____

_____

_____

_____

_____

_____

_____

_____

_____

_____

_____

_____

_____

_____

_____

_____

_____

_____

_____

_____

MY IDEAL SNOWBOUND CHRISTMAS IN THE CAR MUST INCLUDE . . .

_____

_____

_____

_____

_____

_____

_____

_____

_____

_____

_____

THE OUTFIT I WOULD CONSTRUCT OUT OF SCHOOL SUPPLIES AND/OR TRASH IN ORDER TO WIN MY SATURDAY DETENTION FASHION SHOW WOULD FEATURE . . .

_____

_____

_____

_____

_____

_____

_____

_____

_____

_____

_____

_____

_____

_____

_____

_____

IF I HAD CHILI DIARRHEA, THE HARDEST CHALLENGE I COULD FACE WOULD BE . . .

_____

_____

_____

_____

_____

_____

_____

_____

_____

_____

_____

_____

_____

_____

_____

_____

_____

_____

IF TWO-BUTTED GOATS ARE REAL, THEN I THINK THIS ANIMAL SHOULD ALSO BE REAL (TO BE FRIENDS WITH THE TWO-BUTTED GOAT) . . .

_____

_____

_____

_____

_____

_____

_____

_____

_____

_____

_____

_____

_____

_____

_____

_____

_____

_____

IF I RAN AWAY BECAUSE I SUPPOSEDLY HAVE A "CAVITY" THAT "NEEDS FILLING," MY GO-BAG WOULD INCLUDE . . .

_____

_____

_____

_____

_____

_____

_____

_____

_____

_____

_____

_____

_____

_____

_____

_____

_____

_____

THE HISTORICAL EVENT THAT I WOULD LIKE TO DO A PROJECT ON AT SCHOOL, WHICH WOULD INVOLVE BOTH MUSIC AND DANGEROUS AMOUNTS OF ELECTRICITY, IS . . .

_____

_____

_____

_____

_____

_____

_____

_____

_____

_____

_____

_____

_____

_____

_____

_____

_____

_____

TO WIN A JAWBREAKER FROM MY BROTHER OR SISTER, I WOULD BE WILLING TO . . .

_____

_____

_____

_____

_____

_____

_____

_____

_____

_____

_____

_____

_____

_____

_____

_____

_____

THE ANIMALS THAT I THINK HAVE THE MOST PAINTING-WORTHY ANUSES ARE . . .

IN MY FANTASY WHERE A COW KISSES ME, THIS IS WHAT I SAY TO IT FIRST . . .

_____

_____

_____

_____

_____

_____

_____

_____

_____

_____

_____

_____

_____

_____

_____

_____

_____

_____

_____

_____

THE BEST DAY I COULD HAVE WITH MY TINY FRIENDLY LEG HAIRS WOULD INCLUDE . . .

_____

_____

_____

_____

_____

_____

_____

_____

_____

_____

_____

_____

_____

_____

_____

_____

_____

IF I WERE STUCK IN A GIANT TAMMY HEAD WITH TAMMY LARSEN, I WOULD GET REAL AND TELL HER . . .

_____

_____

_____

_____

_____

_____

_____

_____

_____

_____

_____

_____

_____

_____

_____

IF I SUSPECTED THAT MY THUNDERGIRL TROOP HAD A MOLE, HERE IS HOW I WOULD SMOKE HER OUT . . .

_____

_____

_____

_____

_____

_____

_____

_____

_____

_____

_____

_____

_____

_____

_____

_____

_____

MY CONTRIBUTION TO THE HORMONE-IUMS SONGBOOK OF STANDARDS WOULD BE THIS SONG ABOUT EVERY TEEN'S STRUGGLE WITH . . .

THE PERSON I'D MOST LIKE TO GLUE TO A TOILET, AND WHY, IS . . .

_____

_____

_____

_____

_____

_____

_____

_____

_____

_____

_____

_____

_____

_____

_____

_____

_____

_____

_____

THE NON-BATHROOM-RELATED QUESTION
I'D ASK AN ASTRONAUT IS . . .

HERE ARE MY SLUGGY SUGGESTIONS FOR NEW BUROBU CHARACTERS . . .

_____

_____

_____

_____

_____

_____

_____

_____

_____

_____

_____

_____

_____

_____

_____

_____

_____

_____

MY SUPERCOOL NEW "NATURE NAME" WOULD BE . . .

_____

_____

_____

_____

_____

_____

_____

_____

_____

_____

_____

_____